Big-mouth Frog

Naomi Thornton
and André Amstutz

GRAFTON BOOKS

A Division of the Collins Publishing Group

LONDON GLASGOW
TORONTO SYDNEY AUCKLAND

Help Your Child To Write

All children love scribbling; turning scribbling into writing is easier than you think. These books will help you to help your child to write. Each one teaches a specific group of letters but you don't need to buy them all. The whole alphabet and practice patterns are printed at the end of all of them.

At first it is best to enjoy the stories and the pictures for themselves. Then, when the child knows the stories, you can use the characters and events to help him learn to write.

Here are some tips:
1. Have ready lots of paper (the books are not for writing in) and any kind of pencil, pen, felt-tip or crayon.
2. Only practise writing skills when your child is relaxed and in the mood. Respond to his need to learn, not your urge to teach.
3. Holding the pencil correctly like the child in the picture is a first step. Reverse the picture for a left-handed child.
4. All the books start with patterns. These are merely 'rhythmic scribbles' to be repeated until the child can draw them with ease. Each one gives practice in the movements needed for certain letters.

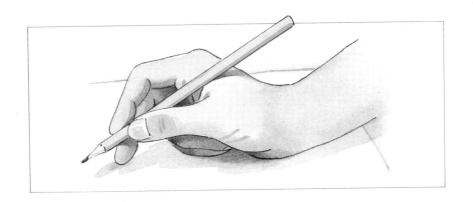

5. It is better for the child to repeat the patterns freely in his own style than to reproduce them accurately but unnaturally.
6. Don't worry about speed. The child will learn best at his own pace.
7. Watching you enjoy the patterns and letters he makes will be more fun for the child than working alone.
8. Remember, there's no need for paper. You can draw letters in the air, in the dust on the sideboard, in sand or on steamed-up windows.
9. When your child knows some letters, help him to use them. When he names an object, get him to write its name down. Get him to label his dog, his bed, his brother, his cup, his jumper. You name it, he can write it. And he'll have fun doing so.

Who's this hopping through the jungle?

Draw the jungle shapes like this:

The big-mouth frog
Was very proud
And his voice was
Very loud

He liked to know
What others ate
And asked each
Creature that he met

One day he met a harvest mouse
Sound asleep inside his house

'Who are you?' he asked the mouse
'And what do you like to eat?'

'I'm a HARVEST MOUSE and I eat
ripe corn,' said the mouse

'I'm a **BIG-MOUTH FROG**,' said the frog

Write HARVEST MOUSE in big
letters like this:

HARVEST MOUSE

Next day he met a lazy lizard
Snoozing in the sun

'Who are you?' asked the big-mouth
frog, 'and what is it that you eat?'

'I'm a LAZY LIZARD and I eat fat flies,' said the lizard

'I'm a **BIG-MOUTH FROG**,' said the frog

Write LAZY LIZARD in big letters like this:

LAZY LIZARD

The big-mouth frog
Met a big black bird
And spoke to him
In these loud words

'Who are you?
What do you eat?'

'I'm a BLACK JACKDAW and I eat
what I can,' said the bird

I'm a
BIG-MOUTH
FROG

Write BLACK JACKDAW in big
letters like this:
BLACK JACKDAW

The big-mouth frog
Next met a snake
Sliding slowly
By the lake

'Who are you?' asked the big-mouth
frog, 'and what do you like to eat?'

'I'm a PURPLE PYTHON,' hissed the snake, 'and my favourite food is mice.'

'I'm a **BIG-MOUTH FROG**,' said the big-mouth frog

Write PURPLE PYTHON in big letters like this:

PURPLE PYTHON

Swimming past
Was a rainbow trout
Who stopped to hear
The big frog shout

Who are you?
What do you eat?

'I'm a RAINBOW TROUT and I eat small shrimps,' said the fish

'I'm a **BIG-MOUTH FROG**,' boasted the frog

Write RAINBOW TROUT in big letters like this:

RAINBOW TROUT

A quick brown fox
Peered from his lair
And at the big-mouth frog
Did stare

'Who are you?
What do you eat?' asked the frog

'I'm a QUICK BROWN FOX,' said the fox, 'and I eat **BIG-MOUTH FROGS**'

What do you eat?

Write QUICK BROWN FOX in big letters like this:

QUICK BROWN FOX

'Oh,' squeaked the big-mouth frog in a tiny voice. 'You don't see many of those about do you?'

Write **BIG-MOUTH FROG** in big letters, and big-mouth frog in small letters, like this:

BIG-MOUTH FROG
big-mouth frog

Practise the patterns, letters and numbers

ABCDEFGH
IJKLMNOPQ
RSTUVWXYZ

abcdefghij
klmnopqrs
tuvwxyz

1 2 3 4 5 6 7
8 9 10

Grafton Books
A Division of the Collins Publishing Group
8 Grafton Street, London W1X 3LA

Published by Grafton Books 1986
Copyright © André Amstutz 1986

British Library Cataloguing in Publication Data
Thornton, Naomi
  Big-mouth Frog. – (Help Your Child To Write; 6)
  1. English language – Alphabet – Juvenile
literature.
  I. Title II. Amstutz, André III. Series
  421'.1   PE1155
  ISBN 0-246-12942-5 (Hardback)
  ISBN 0-583-31000-1 (Paperback)

Printed in Spain by Graficas Reunidas